FIRST
NATURE
Activity
BOOK

ANGELA WILKES

DK

DK Publishing

Previously published as *My First Nature Book*

LONDON, NEW YORK, MELBOURNE, MUNICH, and DELHI

Art editor Chris Scollen
Photography Dave King
Senior designer Neville Graham
Senior editors Marie Greenwood,
Sue Nicholson
Production Amy Bennett

DK Delhi
Senior Editor Glenda Fernandes
Senior Designer Shefali Upadhyay
Designer Mini Dhawan
DTP Designer Harish Aggarwal

First American Edition published in 1990
under the title *My First Nature Book*
This edition published in the United States in 2007 by
DK Publishing
375 Hudson Street
New York, New York 10014

07 08 09 10 10 9 8 7 6 5 4 3 2 1
MD371 - 10/06

A catalog record for this book is available from the
Library of Congress.

ISBN 978-0-7566-2581-8

Reproduced by Media Development
and Printing Ltd, UK
Printed and bound by Leo Paper Products Ltd, China

**Discover more at
www.dk.com**

CONTENTS

NATURE IN PICTURES

My First Nature Book is full of interesting things to do that will help
you to find out more about nature. Simple step-by-step instructions
show you what to do and there are photographs of everything you
need to collect and of the finished projects. At the back of the book
you can find tear-out sheets of blotting paper. Use them to
sprout seeds (see page 14) or press flowers (see page 36).

How to use this book

Equipment
These illustrated checklists
show you which pieces of
equipment to have ready
before you start a project.

The things you need
The things to collect for each
project are shown clearly,
to help you check you have
everything you need.

Step-by-step
Step-by-step photographs
and clear instructions show
you exactly what to do at
every stage of the project.

A TERRARIUM GARDEN

You can create a mossy garden in your home
by growing things in a terrarium. Terrariums
keep in a lot of moisture and are good
for plants that like to grow in damp
places. Any kind of big bottle will
work, as long as it has a wide neck.
Look for mosses, ferns, and lichen
in shady woodland. Here you can
see how to plant them and on the
following page is the finished terrarium.

EQUIPMENT

Pitcher of water
Big spoon

You will need

Different types of moss

Small pebbles or gravel

Small ferns

A big glass bottle

Peat-based potting soil

Pieces of charcoal

Lichen-covered twigs or bark

MAKING THE TERRARIUM

1. Spoon a layer of pebbles or
gravel into the bottom of the
bottle. Add a thin layer of
charcoal, to keep the soil sweet.

2. Cover the pebbles and
charcoal with a deep layer of
potting soil. Pat the soil down
with a spoon.

3. Dig a small hole for the first
plant, using the spoon. Gently
pick up the plant, as shown, and
lower it into the bottle.

4. Cover the plant's roots with
potting soil, then press the soil
down firmly all around the
plant, using the spoon.

5. Dig a shallow hollow for a
clump of moss. Lay the moss in
the hollow and gently pat down
the soil around it.

6. Plant everything in this way,
arranging it as prettily as you
can. Then carefully pour about
a cupful of water into the bottle.

28

29

Things to remember

- Read the instructions before you begin. Some projects need to be done outdoors and some indoors.
- Put on an apron or old shirt and roll up your sleeves.
- Cover your work table with paper before you start a project.

- Gather together everything you need before you start.
- Follow the Country Code on page 48.
- Don't forget to water your plants and take good care of your animals.
- When you have finished a project, put everything away.

Collecting outdoors
The pictures of things to collect are only a guideline. The things you find may not look exactly the same.

The final results
Large pictures show you what finished projects look like, making it easy for you to copy them.

Aftercare
Many of the projects have step-by-step instructions showing you how to care for your plants or creatures.

WORLD IN A BOTTLE

Mosses and ferns are happiest in damp, shady places, so put the terrarium in a cool place where the light is good, but not bright. It is best to avoid direct sunlight.

Once you have made the terrarium, it should require very little looking after. You can see what to do on the opposite page.

Watch the mosses and ferns to see how they grow or change. In spring, the mosses may grow tiny, grasslike stems with capsules on them. These capsules contain the mosses' spores, which are like seeds. You can see three different types of moss with spore capsules at the bottom of the terrarium here. Ferns also produce spore capsules. They are usually on the undersides of the leaves.

Small fern

Twig covered with lichen. Although moss and lichen look alike, they are not related. Lichen is a special type of fungus.

EQUIPMENT

Scissors

Spray bottle

Moss with spore capsules

Maidenhair fern

Potting soil

Watering the plants

Your terrarium will require very little watering. Just spray it with water occasionally to keep the potting soil moist.

Pruning

Keep an eye on the condition of your plants. Snip off any dead leaves or pieces of fern with a small pair of scissors.

Open or closed?

Leave the terrarium open until there are no drops of water left on the inside of the glass. Then you can put the lid on.

Moss with spore capsules

Moss

NATURE SPOTTER'S KIT

Finding out about nature is all about using your eyes. The more carefully you look at things, the more you will find out. It helps to make notes of everything you see. You will also need to collect things, so that you can compare them. Here are the basic things you will need for your nature expeditions.

Small envelopes, for collecting seeds

Plastic bags and ties, for plant specimens

Rubber bands

Sticky labels, for labeling your finds

Small magnifying glass

Containers with holes in their lids or with muslin covers, for collecting insects

Tweezers, for picking up delicate objects

Pencil, for making notes

Pencil sharpener

String

Scissors

Paintbrush, for
picking up
caterpillars

Colored pencils

Nature diary (see page 46)

A NATURE MUSEUM

Your nature collections will look impressive if displayed well so why not make your own nature showcases to show off the interesting things you find? Here you can find out how to make a simple showcase, and on the next page, how to display a collection in the finished showcase.

EQUIPMENT

Pencil

Scissors

Ruler

Pen

You will need

Glue stick

Cotton squares

Clean sand

MAKING THE SHOWCASE

Glue three of the matchboxes together, side by side, in a row. Glue the other three matchboxes together in the same way.

Glue the two rows of three matchboxes together. Since each matchbox has a partition, you will now have 12 compartments.

If you want to make a bigger compartment, glue down the partition in the middle of one of the matchboxes.

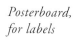

*Posterboard,
for labels*

*Thick,
colored
posterboard*

Six empty household-sized boxes of matches

Cut a piece of posterboard about 1 in (3 cm) wider and 1 in (3 cm) longer than the showcase*. Glue the showcase in the center of it.

Put a thin layer of cotton into each compartment in the showcase. You could use sand for a showcase of a seaside collection.

For labels, cut out rectangles of posterboard. Fold them in half and glue them to the partitions between the matchboxes.

* Ask an adult to help you.

9

NATURE SHOWCASES

Use your nature showcases to show off your most treasured finds. You may have a special collection of feathers, stones, or leaves. Or you may have a seaside or woodland collection. Arrange your exhibits so that similar things are grouped together and label them, if you can.

Rock collection

Look for rocks and pebbles on a beach or riverbank, or on a mountain. You can find them in all colors and with all kinds of patterns. Look them up in a book to find out what they are called.

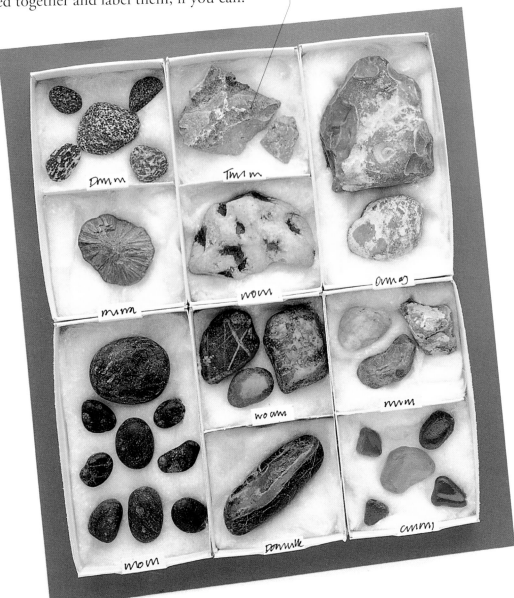

Beachcomber's showcase

Beachcombing can reward you with all kinds of treasures for a showcase. The best place to look is along the high tide mark, especially after a storm. You can find shells in all shapes and sizes, seaweeds, and strange pieces of driftwood.

When you get home, clean your finds under a running faucet with an old toothbrush. Let them dry thoroughly before putting them in your showcase. Continue the seaside theme by lining the showcase with sand, rather than with cotton.

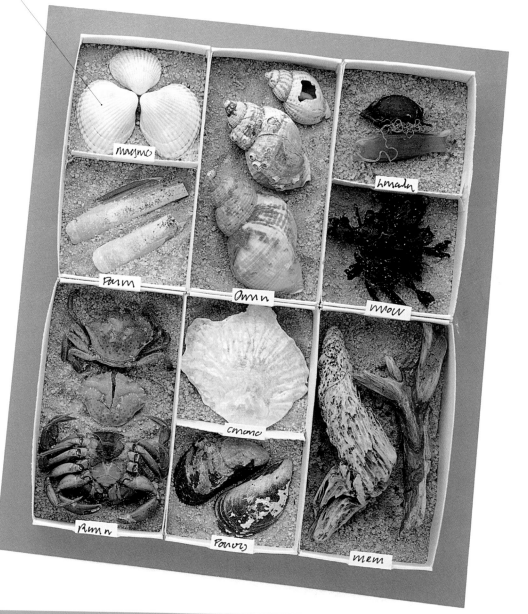

COLLECTING SEEDS

Seeds come in all shapes and sizes. Some are as fine as dust and others look like stones. Some are encased in a juicy fruit; others have their own parachutes. Many flowers, trees, vegetables, fruits, and grasses grow from seeds. See how many different kinds of seeds you can collect. Below are some to look for.

Seeds to collect

Tree seeds

The best time to collect tree seeds is early fall, when they have just fallen from the trees. If you leave it too late, many seeds will have been eaten by birds and animals.

Acorns (from oak trees)

EQUIPMENT

Scissors

Envelopes   *Pencil*

Maple seeds

Horse chestnuts

Seeds in pinecones

Grass seed and grains

Collect different types of seeds from wild grasses or from grains like wheat.

Flower seeds

Look for flower seeds once the petals have died and a seed head has formed.

Thistledown

Wheat

Wild grasses

Poppy seeds

12

Vegetable seeds

All the different kinds of dried beans and peas are seeds.
Soak them for 24 hours before planting them.

Pinto beans   *Black-eyed beans*   *Adzuki beans*   *Kidney beans*

Fruit seeds

Cut fruit in half to find the seeds*. Some
types of fruit have seeds and others pits.

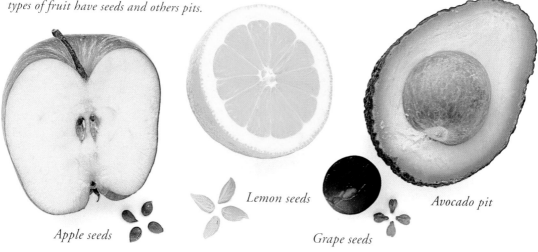

Lemon seeds

Avocado pit

Apple seeds   *Grape seeds*

HARVESTING FLOWER SEEDS

Cut a flower when the petals have died. Hold the flower upside down and shake the seeds on to a piece of paper.

Fold the piece of paper as shown and pour the flower seeds into a small envelope. Use one envelope for each type of seed.

Seal the envelope and label it clearly. Keep it in a dark, dry drawer if you are keeping the seeds to plant in spring.

*Be careful with sharp knives. Ask an adult to help you.

SPROUTING SEEDS

Plant some of the seeds you
have collected and watch
how they grow. Most seeds
will sprout if they have
enough light, air, and water.
On the right you can find
out how to plant seeds and
pits. Turn the page to see
how they grow.

You will need

For growing beans

Large dried beans*

Blotting paper—
use the sheets at the
back of the book.

For cress heads

Watercress seeds

For planting seeds

*Egg
shells*

*Large plastic
bags and ties*

Pits or seeds

Plant labels

Cotton ball

Potting soil

EQUIPMENT

Scissors

Pencil

Bowl

Knife

Jam jar *Flower pots* *Paint box*

Trowel *Jar of water*

* You can use any kind of dried bean.

CRESS HEADS

Draw or paint a simple face on each of the broken egg shells. Stand the egg shell faces in an egg carton, to keep them steady.

Dip balls of cotton in a bowl of water so that they are completely soaked. Fill the egg shells with wet cotton balls.

Sprinkle watercress seeds over the cotton balls. Put the eggs on a window sill and wait for a few days. Keep the cotton balls moist.

SHOOTING BEANS

Cut out a piece of blotting paper tall enough to fill your jam jar from top to bottom and long enough to go all around it.

Roll the blotting paper into a narrow tube and slide it into the jam jar. The blotting paper will open out to fill the jar.

Push a few beans down between the paper and the jar. Pour a little water into the jar, then put it on a window sill.

PLANTING PITS AND SEEDS

Put some potting soil in a bowl and water it to make it moist. Stir well with a trowel. Fill some small pots with the potting soil.

Plant different pits or seeds in each pot. Push them half an inch (1 cm) into the soil. Label each pot to say what it contains.

Put each flower pot inside a polythene bag and tie the top*. Put the pots in a warm place and wait to see which seeds sprout.

* The polythene bags act like mini-greenhouses or incubators.

WATCH SEEDS GROW

Look at your pits, seeds, and beans every day and you will be able to watch each stage of their growth up close. You will find that some things grow very quickly, but others take longer. Remember to water your seeds and seedlings if they look dry. It is also a good idea to turn them regularly, to help them grow straight. All plants are delicate, so treat them with care and they will grow healthy and strong.

PITS AND SEEDS

Here you can see some tree seeds and marrow seeds growing. The tree seeds were planted in the fall and kept in a cool place all winter. The marrow seeds were planted 10 days before the picture was taken.

Baby tree

Baby tree

Marrow seedlings

CRESS HEADS

Watch how the little faces grow green hair! Keep the cotton balls moist and the watercress will take about 10 days to grow. Then you can cut it and add it to salads or egg-salad sandwiches.

SHOOTING BEANS

Here you can see how a bean grows. First, the bean swells and the hard outer skin splits (1). Next, a tiny root appears (2).

The root grows downward and a shoot starts to emerge (3). The shoot then grows upward. Rootlets begin to grow out from the root and the plant produces leaves (4).

From now on, the bean plant grows fast (5). When it is too big for the jar, plant it in a pot or in the garden, with a stick to support it.

1.

2.

3.

4.

5.

17

FEEDING THE BIRDS

Feeding the birds in winter helps them to survive when food is scarce and gives you a chance to watch them. Here you can find out how to make a filling bird suet and peanut kebabs. The quantities given for the suet will fill a small yogurt cup. Turn the page to see other tasty ideas for your birds' menu.

Several tablespoons of any of these:

Oatmeal

Leftover cooked vegetables

You will need

4 Tbsp shortening

Birdseed

Cooked rice

Mixed nuts

Brown breadcrumbs

Small twig

Grated cheese

EQUIPMENT

Scissors

Mixing bowl

Big needle*

Wooden spoon   *Small saucepan*

Yogurt cup

* Use a blunt-tipped darning needle

Big pinecone

For peanut kebabs

String *Peanuts in their shells and any other nuts*

MAKING THE SUET

1. Mix the scraps together in the bowl. Set aside some birdseed. Ask an adult to melt shortening in a saucepan over a low heat.

2. Pour the melted shortening over the mixture in the bowl and stir everything together well with a wooden spoon.

3. Spoon the suet mixture into the yogurt cup. Push a twig into the suet, then leave the suet to harden.

4. When the suet has set, pull it out of the yogurt cup by the twig and roll it in birdseed. Tie a piece of string to the twig.

Pinecone feeder

Push bird suet into the cracks between the open scales of a big pinecone, then hang the cone from a piece of string.

Peanut kebab

Make holes in peanut shells and other nuts with a big needle*. Knot one end of a piece of string, then thread the nuts on to it.

* Be careful with the needle.

19

BIRDS' MENU

Here are some ideas for simple bird feeders and tidbits. Hang the feeders where you can watch them easily, and make sure they are out of reach of cats. Keep a record in your nature diary (see page 46) of all the birds that use the feeders. Do the same birds keep coming back, and do they have regular feeding times?

SCRAP BAG
You can make a very simple feeder for the birds from a fine mesh fruit bag*. Fill it with nuts or bird suet, then tie the top with a piece of string and hang it up.

COCONUT BELL
Hang half a coconut upside down from a piece of string and agile birds will peck out all the coconut. When the shell is empty, fill it with bird suet.

BELL TREAT
This is the finished bird suet you saw how to make on the last two pages.

*Usually available at supermarkets.

PEANUT KEBAB
String up your peanut kebab (see page 19) and watch the birds break open the nuts.

FEEDING LOG
You will need an adult to help you make this. Ask him or her to drill holes in the log and to screw a hook in the top. Fill the holes with bird suet and hang up the log. Woodpeckers may come to peck out the suet.

PINECONE FEEDER
This is the feeder you saw how to make on page 19. Watch the birds sway from it as they feed.

TREE PRINTS

A tree's bark is its skin and, like human fingerprints, no two trees have identical bark. Different types of tree also have different bark, and bark also changes as a tree grows older. You can keep a record of what sort of bark a tree has by taking a rubbing of it. This way you can build up a file of "tree prints." Here you can see what to do.

Thumbtack

You will need

Thick wax crayons

Masking tape

Construction paper, 12 in by 12 in (30 cm by 30 cm)

WHAT TO DO

Choose a tree with fairly smooth bark, with no moss or lichen growing on it. Tape or tack a piece of paper firmly to the tree.

Using the flat side of a wax crayon, rub firmly up and down the paper. Keep doing this until the paper is covered.

Untape the paper from the tree. Write the name of the tree on the back of the paper, if you know what it is called.

THE FINISHED RUBBINGS
Each rubbing looks completely different. Some have bold, dramatic stripes. Others are dappled or spotted, like a leopard's fur.

23

FROM BUD TO LEAF

Most broadleaved trees have no leaves in winter and look lifeless. But look closely at some twigs and you will see that each one is already covered in tiny buds. These buds contain the beginnings of next year's shoots, leaves, and flowers. You can make buds open early by cutting some twigs and bringing them indoors. Put them in a jar of water and you can watch how they burst into life. The best twigs to try are horse chestnut, forsythia, and magnolia. Here you can see how horse chestnut buds open.

OPENING BUDS

Side twig

Each fat bud is covered with sticky scales that protect it. Inside the scales are tightly packed new stems and leaves.

The buds swell and begin to burst out of the scales.

Leaf scar from last year.

This is a girdle scar. You can tell how old the twig is by counting the girdle scars.

24

The new leaves inside the buds begin to unfurl. They are covered in protective fluffy down.

Tiny flower covered in down.

The stems start to grow and the leaves open out to the light.

Flower

Flower

New shoot

The bud scales curl back. In a few weeks they will drop off, leaving a girdle scar.

CREEPY CRAWLY PIT TRAPS

You do not have to go far to find animals to watch. There are tiny creatures all around you in your yard or park. To find out what they are, set up simple pit traps. Check the traps often and write down what you find, to keep a record of local wildlife.

You will need (for each trap)

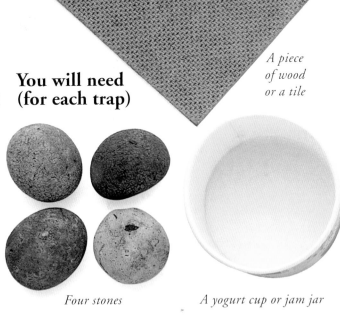

A piece of wood or a tile

Four stones

A yogurt cup or jam jar

EQUIPMENT

Nature diary

Pencil

Trowel

Dish

Saucer

Food for bait

A cube of cheese

Cookie crumbs

A piece of apple

A piece of meat

SETTING UP A PIT TRAP

Dig a hole in the yard. Sink the yogurt cup into it, so that its rim is level with the soil. Fill in soil around the edges of the cup.

Drop a small piece of cheese or other bait into the yogurt cup trap. The smell of the bait will attract small creatures to the trap.

Put the four stones around the top of the yogurt pot. Lay the piece of wood across them to make a protective cover for the trap.

INSECT PATROL

Empty the creatures in the trap into a dish. Write down what you have caught in your nature diary, then set the creatures free.

Try setting several traps, using different baits, such as meat, fish, or fruit. Do different types of bait attract different creatures?

To see which creatures live where, sink traps in different places: in a flowerbed or vegetable garden, for example.

The pit trap

Here you can see right into a pit trap. Small creatures have fallen into it and cannot climb out up the slippery sides. Check your traps every few hours, to see whether any creatures have fallen into them.

The cover of the pit trap protects the insects inside it from bright sun, the rain, or any hungry animals on the prowl.

Stone

Yogurt cup

Ground level

Bait

Creatures caught in the trap

27

A TERRARIUM GARDEN

You can create a mossy garden in your home by growing things in a terrarium. Terrariums keep in a lot of moisture and are good for plants that like to grow in damp places. Any kind of big bottle will work, as long as it has a wide neck. Look for mosses, ferns, and lichen in shady woodland. Here you can see how to plant them and on the following page is the finished terrarium.

EQUIPMENT

Pitcher of water

Big spoon

You will need

Different types of moss

Small pebbles or gravel

A big glass bottle

Peat-based potting soil

MAKING THE TERRARIUM

1. Spoon a layer of pebbles or gravel into the bottom of the bottle. Add a thin layer of charcoal to keep the soil sweet.

2. Cover the pebbles and charcoal with a deep layer of potting soil. Pat the soil down with a spoon.

3. Dig a small hole for the first plant, using the spoon. Gently pick up the plant, as shown, and lower it into the bottle.

4. Cover the plant's roots with potting soil, then press the soil down firmly all around the plant, using the spoon.

5. Dig a shallow hollow for a clump of moss. Lay the moss in the hollow and gently pat down the soil around it.

6. Plant everything in this way, arranging it as prettily as you can. Then carefully pour about a cupful of water into the bottle.

Small ferns

Pieces of charcoal

Lichen-covered twigs or bark

29

WORLD IN A BOTTLE

Mosses and ferns are happiest in damp, shady places, so put the terrarium in a cool place where the light is good, but not bright. It is best to avoid direct sunlight.

Once you have made the terrarium, it should require very little looking after. You can see what to do on the opposite page.

Watch the mosses and ferns to see how they grow or change. In spring, the mosses may grow tiny, grasslike stems with capsules on them. These capsules contain the mosses' spores, which are like seeds. You can see three different types of moss with spore capsules at the bottom of the terrarium here. Ferns also produce spore capsules. They are usually on the undersides of the leaves.

Small fern

Twig covered with lichen. Although moss and lichen look alike, they are not related. Lichen is a special type of fungus.

EQUIPMENT

Scissors

Spray bottle

Moss with spore capsules

30

Maidenhair fern

Potting soil

Moss with spore capsules

Moss

Watering the plants

Your terrarium will require very little watering. Just spray it with water occasionally to keep the potting soil moist.

Pruning

Keep an eye on the condition of your plants. Snip off any dead leaves or pieces of fern with a small pair of scissors.

Open or closed?

Leave the terrarium open until there are no drops of water left on the inside of the glass. Then you can put the lid on.

CATERPILLAR HOUSE

Keep some caterpillars and you may be lucky enough to see how they change into butterflies. Look for caterpillars on the leaves of plants and bushes in spring and summer. The plant they are on is probably their food plant, so pick plenty of leaves for them to eat. Here and on pages 34 and 35 you can find out how to make a home for your wiggly pets.

You will need

Caterpillars

EQUIPMENT

Cutting board

Scissors

Spray bottle

Paintbrush

MAKING THE CATERPILLAR HOUSE

Ask an adult to cut a big hole out of the lid of the plastic container, leaving just a bit of the lid inside the rim.

Cut out a piece of muslin that is big enough to cover the top of the container and overlap the edges all the way around.

Line the container with over-lapping pieces of paper towel or tissues. Spray them lightly with water, to dampen them.

A large plastic
container

Paper towel
or tissues

A big piece
of muslin

The leaves your
caterpillars eat

Small twigs

Lay the food leaves (leaves from
the plant on which you found
the caterpillars) in the container.
Lay the twigs on top.

One at a time, gently pick up the
caterpillars on the paintbrush
and put them carefully on the
leaves in the container.

Lay the muslin over the top of
the container. Then push the lid
down over the muslin to hold it
firmly in place.

Turn the page to see what to do next. 33

FROM CATERPILLAR TO BUTTERFLY

Here is the caterpillar house without its lid, so that you can see inside. You will be able to watch your caterpillars change into chrysalises when they are fully grown, and later into butterflies. Keep the caterpillar house in a quiet place away from direct sunlight. Caterpillars eat a lot, so clean out the house and give them fresh leaves to eat every day. On the right you can find out what to do.

Paper towel

CATERPILLAR FOOD
The caterpillars shown here eat passionflower leaves and nothing else. Each type of caterpillar has its own food plant, so it is very important that you give them the right leaves to eat. These are usually the leaves on which you found them in the wild.

CATERPILLARS
Caterpillars are very delicate. Do not prod or disturb them, because you could easily harm them. As caterpillars grow bigger, they outgrow their skins and molt, so do not worry if you see a caterpillar wriggle out of its skin. Most caterpillars molt several times during their lives.

Plastic container

34

THE CHRYSALIS STAGE

This is a chrysalis (or pupa). A caterpillar changes into a chrysalis when it is fully grown. The chrysalis is its last skin change before it becomes a butterfly (or moth). The chrysalis may form on a twig or on the side of the container. Try not to disturb it. You may have to wait a long time before the butterfly emerges.

Twig

Leaves

BUTTERFLIES

When a butterfly first emerges from a chrysalis, it will have folded-up wings and look somewhat strange. It will take several hours for its wings to dry and harden. A butterfly is very delicate, so leave it alone and set it free when it is sunny.

CLEANING OUT THE HOUSE

Take the lid off the caterpillar house and carefully lift out everything inside, including the paper towel.

Line the caterpillar house with clean paper towel or tissue and spray it with water to dampen it. Put in fresh food leaves.

Pick up each caterpillar in turn on the paintbrush and put it back in the caterpillar house. Then put the lid back on.

PLANT PRESS

Pressing is a simple but magical way of preserving beautiful flowers and leaves so that they last forever. Flowers with flat faces, like pansies, primroses, and daisies are all easy to press. Pick dry, undamaged flowers and leaves and press them quickly, so that they keep their color*. Here you can find out how to make a simple plant press, and on the next pages you can see how to make pictures and cards.

You will need

Flowers and leaves to press

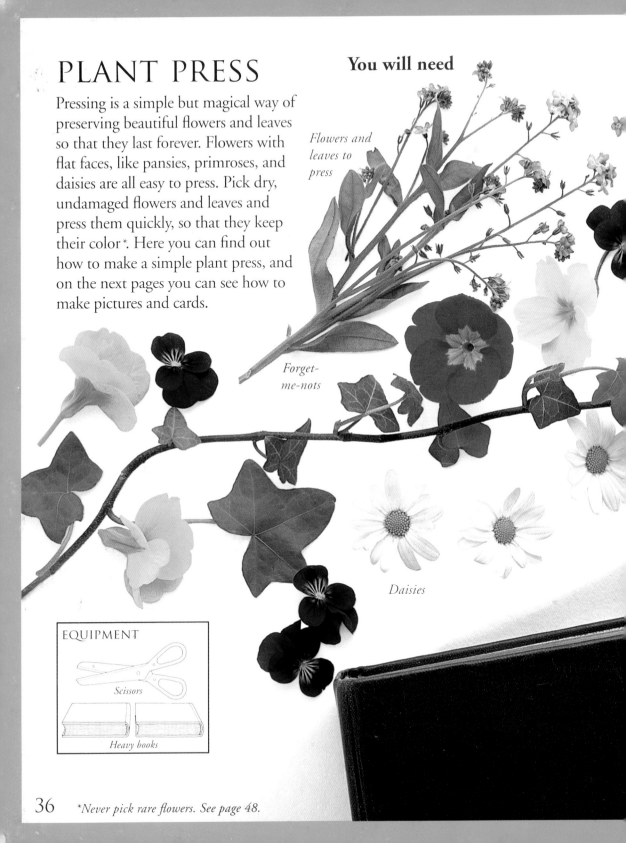

Forget-me-nots

Daisies

EQUIPMENT

Scissors

Heavy books

36   *Never pick rare flowers. See page 48.

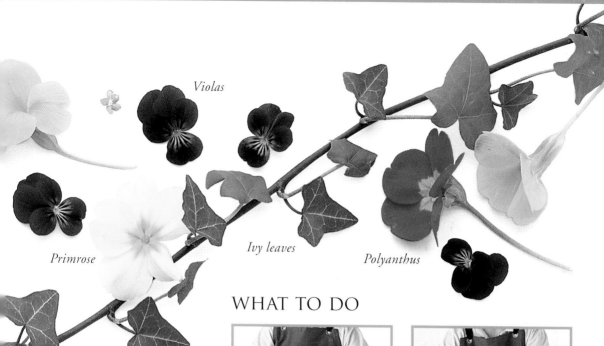

Violas

Ivy leaves

Primrose

Polyanthus

White blotting paper—use the tear-out sheets at the back of the book

Heavy books

WHAT TO DO

1. Open the book. Cut out a piece of blotting paper about the same size as the open book. Fold the paper in half, then open it out.

2. Lay the blotting paper across the book. Arrange the plants flat on the right half of the paper, leaving space between them.

3. Carefully fold the left side of the blotting paper over the plants. Then close the book over the blotting paper*.

4. Put some heavy books or magazines on top of the book, to weigh it down. Leave the plants to dry for at least four weeks.

* To press more plants, do the same thing farther on in the book.

Turn the page to see what to do next. 37

EVERLASTING FLOWERS

After four weeks, your pressed plants should be dry and flat. You can glue them into your nature diary, to keep a record of what you have found, or make pictures with them. Start by making simple pictures with just one or two flowers, then experiment once you have had more practice. Here are some ideas for what you can make with your pressed flowers.

You will need

Posterboard

Cotton swabs

Rubber-based glue

EQUIPMENT

Ruler

Scissors

Pencil

Pressed flowers and leaves

MAKING PICTURES

Measure and draw out the size you want your picture to be on paper or posterboard. Cut the paper out carefully.

Arrange where to put each flower and leaf. Pick up a flower and dab a tiny spot of glue on the back of it.

Gently position the flower where you want it. Do the same with the other flowers, then leave the glue to dry.

FLOWERY IDEAS

You can make your own unique cards, gift tags, or bookmarks using simple arrangements of pressed flowers and leaves.

Picture

Bookmark

Gift tags

A WORM FARM

Worms are busy creatures and play an important role in the garden, keeping the soil in good condition. You can watch what they do by making this simple worm farm. Keep it until you have seen what the worms do, then put them back where you found them.

You will need

*Earthworms**

A large glass jar

Dead leaves

Sand

Sieved garden soil

EQUIPMENT

Trowel

Bowls

Spray bottle

Small bowl

Dark cloth

*The worms should be big, mature ones with a "saddle" around the middle.

MAKING THE WORM FARM

Fill the jar with alternate layers of soil and sand. Make each layer about 1 in (2.5 cm) deep and spray each one with water.

Gently put the worms into the jar, keeping them away from bright light. Five or six worms should be enough for a jar this size.

Cover the top layer of soil with dead leaves. Then cover the whole jar with a dark cloth or put in it a dark place*.

BURROWING WORMS

Leave the worm farm alone for a few days, then take a look at it. Here you can see how the worms have tunneled through the soil and sand, so that the different layers have begun to mix together. They have also dragged the leaves down into the soil, to eat them.

Dead leaves

Soil

Layers of soil
merging

USEFUL WORMS

Worms do not eat all the leaves and plant matter they pull down into the soil. Their leftovers help to enrich the soil and make better growing conditions for plants. The worm tunnels are also useful for plants, because they help to provide air for the plants' roots.

Leaves dragged
down into soil

Sand

Worm tunnels

Worm

* The worms need to be in complete darkness so that they think they are underground.

41

PET WATCHING

You do not need to live on a farm or near a zoo to find out about animals and how they behave. You can learn all kinds of fascinating things by keeping a close watch on the pets you have at home. Your puppy will often behave in exactly the same way as a fox or wolf cub and your kitten will play like a lion cub.

Watch your pets carefully and write down the things you notice in your nature diary (see page 46). What does your pet do and where does it go? How can you tell what mood it is in? Keep your eyes open and you can learn a lot, not only about your pet, but about animals in general. Here are some things to look out for.

TAIL TALK
You can tell a lot about a cat's feelings by its tail. A happy cat walks with its tail held high. An angry cat may swish its tail from side to side. A frightened cat often cowers with its tail tucked between its legs.

EXPRESSIVE FACES
Watch your cat's face, to see what mood it is in. When curious, it will prick up its ears and open its eyes wide. It may also twitch its whiskers. When frightened or angry, it will lay its ears back flat.

PLAY-LEARNING
Playing is how your kitten learns skills that are important in the wild, such as hunting. Kittens love to chase and pounce on interesting new things. Watch how they use their paws to hook things toward them for a closer look.

CAT STOPS
Watch where your cat goes every day. Most cats are creatures of habit and will have their own special lookout posts and places for resting, cleaning, or sunbathing. Your cat will also have its own prowling "territory" and will rarely venture outside it.

DOGGY MOODS

As with people, you can tell a lot about a dog's mood by the expression on its face. Dogs can look questioning or fierce and can even appear to smile. Learn which signs tell you when your dog is happy or sad, or when it wants to play.

NOSEY DOGS

A dog's sense of smell is more sensitive than ours and gives it all kinds of useful information. That is why dogs want to sniff everything wherever they go.

WOOFS AND WHIMPERS

Dogs make a whole range of sounds: whimpers, growls, snarls, and barks. Listen carefully to your dog and learn to recognize the different sounds and what they mean.

BODY LANGUAGE

A dog shows its feelings with its whole body, as well as its face. In particular, it has an expressive tail. Watch how your dog moves and what it does to show what it wants to do.

TRACKING YOUR PETS

An easy way to study animal tracks is to make plaster casts of them and the best places to look for tracks are in mud or wet sand. But before collecting different prints, why not practice by taking casts of your pet's paw prints? Here you can find out what to do.

You will need

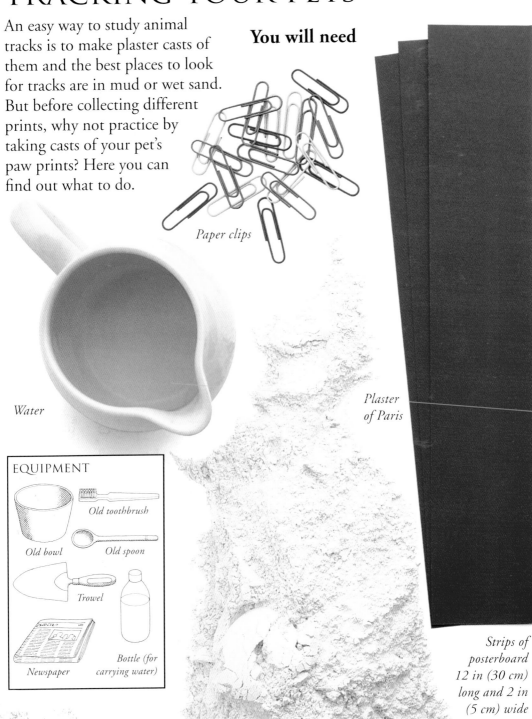

Paper clips

Water

Plaster of Paris

EQUIPMENT

Old toothbrush

Old bowl

Old spoon

Trowel

Newspaper

Bottle (for carrying water)

Strips of posterboard 12 in (30 cm) long and 2 in (5 cm) wide

44

MAKING THE PLASTER CASTS

Find a print in wet mud. Clip a strip of posterboard into a circle to go around the print. Push it into the mud around the print.

Mix the plaster of Paris* in the bowl. Gently pour about 2 in (5 cm) of plaster into the ring. Leave it for 15 minutes, to set.

Dig up the plaster cast and the mud around it. Wrap the cast in newspaper and take it home. Leave it for a day, to set**.

Ask an adult to help you, following the instructions on the packet.
*** Wash the bowl and spoon with warm water as soon as you get home.*

PRINTS IN PLASTER

When the plaster is hard, unclip the posterboard and scrub the cast clean under running water, using an old tooth-brush. The finished cast will be a raised copy of your pet's paw print. Here you can see plaster casts of dog and cat paw prints and of a guinea pig's tracks.

GUINEA PIG PRINT

CAT PAW PRINT

DOG PAW PRINT

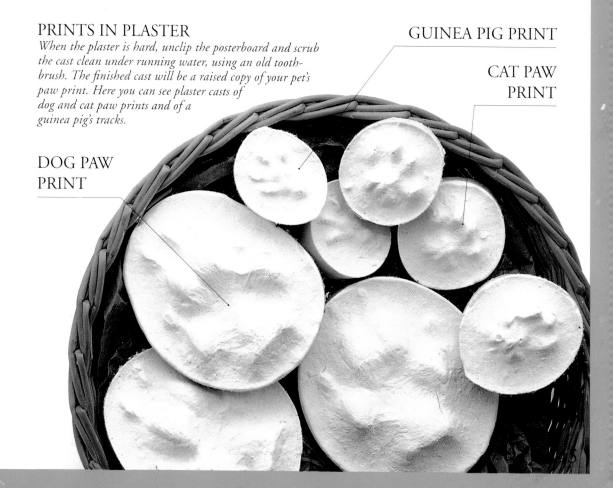

YOUR NATURE DIARY

Keep a nature diary and it will become your own personal record of all the interesting things you see and find. You can use any notebook for your diary, but it is best if it has a hard cover and a ring binding, so that you can open it out flat when you are drawing.

Make notes in your nature diary of everything you see and draw things as often as you can. You can keep records of how your seeds are growing and of what your pets are doing. If you can, label each find in your diary and write down where you found everything.

FACTS FIRST
Start each entry in your diary with the date. Then you could say what the weather has been like and where you have been.

LEAVES AND FLOWERS
Your diary is a good place to keep leaves or flowers that you find. First you must press them (see pages 36 and 37). When they are flat and dry, glue them into the diary.

GROWING THINGS
Keep notes of how your seeds and plants are growing (see pages 14 to 17 for some ideas). Draw each new stage in your seedlings' growth and write down everything that you notice happening.

Sunday, April 9
Sunny day, some clouds. Went to the woods near Grandma's.

Buddleia leaves

Horse chestnut leaf

My bean plant

The roots have tiny roots growing from them. The shoot has reached the top of the paper.

Polyanthus flower from garden.

FINDS

You can glue or tape interesting finds, like these feathers, in your diary. Write down when and where you found them and label them if you know what they are called.

QUICK SKETCHES

Try to draw new birds that you see. You do not have to be good at drawing. Draw two circles—one for the head and one for the body. Add the tail, beak, and legs and a wing, then fill in the colors and details of special markings.

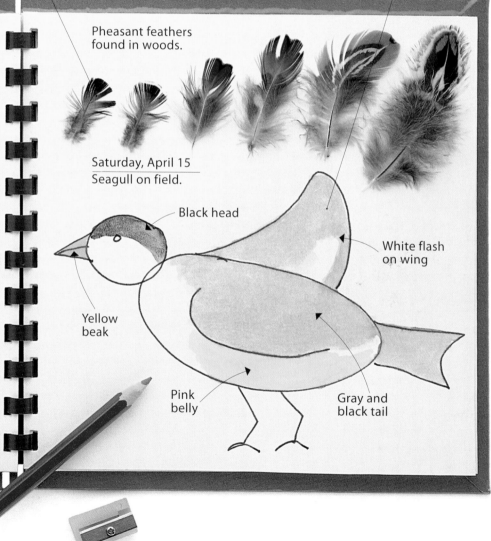

Pheasant feathers found in woods.

Saturday, April 15
Seagull on field.

Black head

White flash on wing

Yellow beak

Pink belly

Gray and black tail

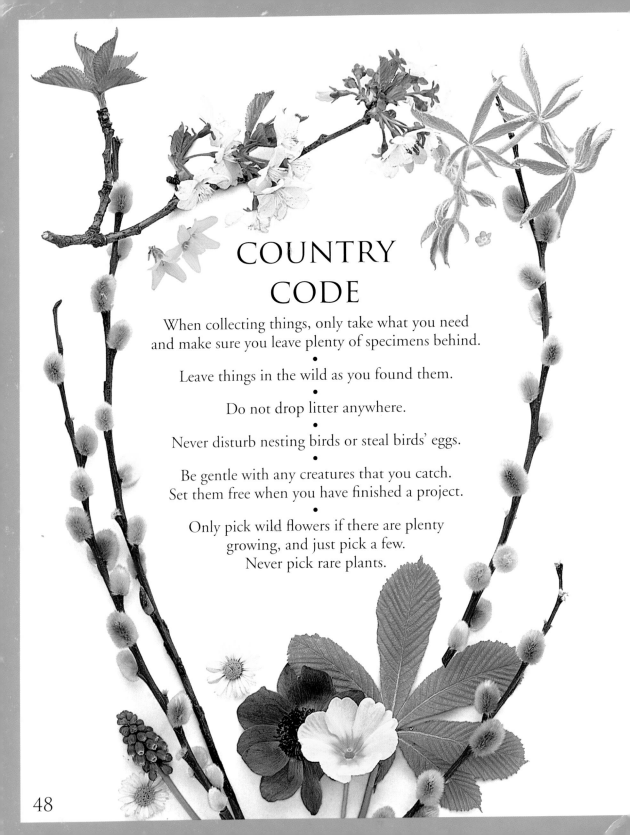

COUNTRY
CODE

When collecting things, only take what you need
and make sure you leave plenty of specimens behind.

•

Leave things in the wild as you found them.

•

Do not drop litter anywhere.

•

Never disturb nesting birds or steal birds' eggs.

•

Be gentle with any creatures that you catch.
Set them free when you have finished a project.

•

Only pick wild flowers if there are plenty
growing, and just pick a few.
Never pick rare plants.